Michael T. Winstanle

An Introduction to
Mark

Don Bosco
Publications

Don Bosco Publications
Thornleigh House, Sharples Park, Bolton BL1 6PQ
United Kingdom

ISBN 978-1-909080-71-3

Front cover photo Sodacan/GNU Free Document License

Printed in Malta by Melita Press

FSC
www.fsc.org
MIX
Paper from responsible sources
FSC® C110322

Contents

Introduction

The Gospel of Mark is the shortest of the four canonical Christian Gospels. Most scripture scholars these days believe that Mark was the first person to write a 'Gospel'; in fact, he was the one who created this literary genre. For centuries the view of Augustine was widely accepted, whereby Mark was thought to have copied and abbreviated the Gospel of Matthew. Things changed in the nineteenth century, when scholars came to realise that in fact it was Mark who wrote first, and he did so probably soon after the fall of Jerusalem and the destruction of the temple in 70CE. A long tradition maintains that he wrote in Rome, and a majority of scholars still accept this view. Others suggest a place nearer to Palestine, like southern Syria. Many attempts have been made over the years to identify Mark; he has been linked with the John Mark of Acts, and with the Mark of the Pauline letters and 1 Peter, but certainty seems elusive. Mark was a very popular Roman name.

For his task, Mark used oral traditions about Jesus which were circulating in the early Christian communities and probably some written traditions too. This material coming from different sources he arranged in the form of a narrative. The storyline after the Jordan baptism at the beginning until the Calvary scene at the end depends not on the historical chronological sequence of Jesus' actual ministry, but on Mark's own creative design.

I believe that it is useful to view all the Gospels from three complementary perspectives: literary, historical and theological. The Gospels are pieces of literature, written by competent writers for a particular clientèle, using the literary techniques of their time. They are the word of God in human language. The evangelists have their own individual style and characteristic traits. Literary techniques are employed like irony, symbolism, inclusion, parallelism. There is a plot, character portrayal, conflict development, the careful use of time and space settings and of movement. The Old Testament is constantly in the background, implicitly and sometimes explicitly.

The Gospels are also historical documents but not in the sense that every detail is factually accurate. Jesus lived in a particular geographical, social, religious, economic and historical setting, in a predominantly Jewish culture which was also influenced by the wider Greco-Roman culture of the Mediterranean basin. The rich diversity of this backcloth is reflected in the Gospels. Many historical issues arise in the narrative and require consideration.

The main purpose of the evangelists is what I would call theological. As a person of deep faith, each of the evangelists seeks to share that faith vision and conviction with others, his readers and hearers. They are preachers and catechists; their work has been described as sermons in story form. They set out to tell us about God and God's offer of salvation and new life; about Jesus—his life, ministry, death and resurrection; about the world we live in; about sin and death, and about discipleship.

The evangelists have their own individual theological perspectives and emphases. They tell the story of Jesus in order to elicit a response from those listening or reading: a response of faith, ongoing conversion, love and commitment. And so, I believe that the key question I need to ask when confronted with a Gospel extract is: what is the theological message, the word from God, which this evangelist is seeking to communicate here? What aspects of the faith of the early Christian community is the author articulating and proclaiming? Moving on from there I seek to discern what the Gospel message is for me, for us today, in our very different world and evolving culture, with its new problems and fresh challenges.

In this small book, I propose to examine Mark's Gospel from a literary perspective and consider the four main 'characters' in the story: Jesus, the twelve disciples, the 'opposition' and the little people or minor characters. To conclude, I will discuss the death and resurrection of Jesus.

Chapter One

Jesus

I would like to begin by looking at the way Mark introduces his story of Jesus. In the opening fifteen verses he provides us with a privileged perspective, giving us the information that will enable us better to understand the whole narrative as it unfolds. From the outset we know more than the participants in the drama. These verses form a kind of prologue. They furnish us with important clues which will enable us to understand the story and the denouement of the action. They give us insight into Jesus' identity, who he is, and what he is up to, what is his mission or role, what is really happening at the deeper level in the course of his ministry.

Mark has no Infancy Narrative like Luke or Matthew, no poetic prologue like John. He opens his Gospel rather abruptly with a statement which expresses his faith stance: "The beginning of the Good News of Jesus Christ, the Son of God." Perhaps echoing the first phrase of Genesis, it serves as a kind of title or heading for the story on which he is embarking, a story which heralds a new creation on the part of God. This story is good news, news intended to make the hearer or reader glad, news which is a cause for rejoicing.

The key figure is introduced immediately. He is the one who brought and proclaimed this news through his preaching and actions. He is also the content of the story, he is the good news, for the author intends to share with his community and others beyond its confines the significance of his presence in the world. This Jesus, Mark confesses, is "the Christ", the Messiah, the anointed one. Rather than his name, 'Christ' designates his role, his mission. And he is the "Son of God". He has a special, unique relationship with God.

A scriptural quotation, which is a prophetic word from God, follows:

> As it is written in the prophet Isaiah, "See, I am sending my messenger ahead of you, who will prepare your way; the voice of one crying out in the wilderness: 'Prepare the way of the Lord, make his paths straight.'"

Although attributed to Isaiah, it is actually a composite citation strategically adapted. God enters the story: in fact, God is behind the whole event of Jesus. Here God speaks off-stage to Jesus, indicating that it is He, God, who sends a messenger ahead of Jesus to prepare his way. God is the initiator, the guide and power behind all that will now take place. The term 'Lord', used constantly for Yahweh in the Septuagint (the Greek Old Testament), is here applied to Jesus. This means that where Jesus is acting, God is acting. 'The way of the Lord' is a phrase often found in Isaiah for the route or road by which God will bring the people back from exile. The term 'way' will be important in Mark's story: 'the way of the Lord' now leads to the cross and eventual vindication; this 'way' becomes the path of discipleship.

The tone and setting change, as, without any mention of his background or earlier history, the messenger arrives on the scene. In the Gospels, John is naturally viewed in his relationship with Jesus. In fact, he was a significant and important figure in his own right. God's messenger is immediately referred to as the 'Baptiser'. The verb means to dip, wash, immerse, soak; this is the distinctive prophetic activity through which he is best known. John quickly won the respect of the ordinary people, who came out from the villages and towns of Judea to find and listen to him. He appears as a nomad prophet and operates independently of institutionalised religion. He seems to have nothing to do with the Jerusalem Temple, its authorities and sacrificial system. Nor does he quote the scriptures. As indicated by God's word, he makes his appearance in the "wilderness". This setting is highly symbolic. In the hindsight of centuries, the time spent in the wilderness during the Exodus came to be viewed rather idealistically as the period of God's (almost honeymoon) closeness with the people in covenant love and liberation, the time of Israel's most intense experiences of God, even though it was also a time of testing, rebellion and punishment. This view was then romantically projected into the future, so that with the passing of the years the expectation developed that God's final saving intervention in the end time would commence in the wilderness, as a kind of new Exodus. So, the wilderness setting suggests that God is about to renew the covenant with Israel, to inaugurate the new age. John seems to have moved up and down the lower Jordan river in the barren land east of Jerusalem towards the Dead Sea.

John was convinced that the root of the crisis of his people was their sinfulness, which was frustrating God's design. There was need for radical change and a fresh start. His baptism was a rite of conversion and forgiveness, signifying a new beginning and a new future. There was something special, something original and innovative about John's baptism. It was different from the self-administered immersion which some scholars believe converts to Judaism were expected to undergo. It differed also from the repeated ritual washing practised in the elite Qumran community, also self-administered. John's baptism was offered to all Jews. It was a one-off event and not repeated. It was not self-administered but administered by him. It stemmed from the recognition that Israel had gone astray, the realisation of the need for conversion, both personal and national. There was an urgency about it.

Repentance and the forgiveness of sins are central to John's proclamation and baptising activity. For him this forgiveness lay in the future, when the "stronger one",[1] whose sandals he was unworthy to untie, would come. It is he who will baptise with the Holy Spirit. The outpouring of the Spirit was expected in God's time of salvation, bringing about complete renewal and restoration. For Mark, John's main role is to be the precursor, to pave the way for the "stronger one", the "coming one", the agent of God's salvation—for Jesus.

---

1 The "mightier one" *(ıschyroteros)* is an attribute which is sometimes applied to God in the Old Testament (2 Sam 22:31; 23:5; Ps 7:12; Isa 40:10; 49:25; 9:6). In Job (22:13; 33:29; 36:22), the "mighty one" is a term for God.

After his description of the Baptist, Mark finally brings Jesus on stage. He journeys from Nazareth in Galilee to the Judean Jordan area and submits to John's baptism. After this episode comes Jesus' testing or temptations. Finally, after the arrest of the Baptist, Jesus embarks on his ministry/mission, with his proclamation of the advent of the Kingdom, and the exhortation to repent and believe. The centrepiece is the baptism. Mark describes the baptism of Jesus as follows:

> In those days Jesus came from Nazareth of Galilee and was baptised by John in the Jordan. And just as he was coming up out of the water, he saw the heavens torn apart and the Spirit descending like a dove on him. And a voice came from heaven, "You are my Son, the Beloved; with you I am well pleased."

The actual baptism is stated, not described; John is the actor and Jesus the recipient. For the evangelist, the baptism itself is not important; the emphasis is placed on the accompanying phenomena, where God is the actor and Jesus the recipient. Mark provides no information about Jesus' earlier life or background. Jesus joins the thronging crowds from Judea and Jerusalem, mentioned earlier, who flock to John for baptism. He expresses his solidarity with them.

Immediately as Jesus emerges from the water, the heavens are 'torn open'. This piece of graphic imagery is a frequent symbol in Jewish literature as a way of indicating that God is about to communicate. "In Mark, then, God has ripped the heavens irrevocably apart at Jesus' baptism, never to shut them again. Through this gracious gash in the universe, he has poured forth his Spirit into the earthly realm."[2] It is like an invisible curtain being pulled back, allowing us to stand in the presence of a different reality. Then the Holy Spirit gently glides down, 'dove-like', and rests upon Jesus. The image is probably intended to evoke the Genesis picture of God's creative Spirit hovering over the waters of chaos at the dawn of time, 'in the beginning', likened by the rabbis to a dove brooding over her young. It suggests that God's creative Spirit is once more active in the world, an activity focused on the person of Jesus. "Jesus Christ and Son of God, the Lord, and the Stronger One, who will dispense the Holy Spirit, has now been gifted with the Spirit."[3] And so he can baptise with the Spirit, as John the Baptist has indicated.

Then the second phenomenon occurs. From heaven "a voice" speaks to Jesus, and in Mark to him alone; there is no hint that anyone else hears it, except the reader: "You are my Son, the Beloved; with you I am well pleased". These words, restating the opening verse of the Gospel, indicate for us the immense significance which the evangelist saw in the event. What is most important here is that it is God who addresses these words to Jesus. God is an actor in the story; and God clearly identifies for the reader who Jesus is; God reveals how he 'thinks' about Jesus. At the outset of the Gospel, God affirms that this Jesus from Nazareth is the specially chosen and favoured one, the only Son, designated as the (Davidic) kingly Messiah, and anointed for mission by the Holy Spirit. If the Isaian text is linked

2 Quoted by both R. Alan Culpepper, *Mark*, (Macon: Smyth and Helwys, 2008), 49, and Francis J. Moloney, *The Gospel of Mark. A Commentary*, (Peabody, MA; Hendrickson, 2002), 36; from Joel Marcus, *Mark 1–8*, (New York; Doubleday, 2000), 165.

3 Moloney, *Mark*, 37.

with later servant passages, it could be that his task is radically interpreted in terms of the Servant of Yahweh; he is to fulfil his role according to a pattern of service and self-emptying.[4]

The evaluation of Jesus as Messiah, Son of God with which Mark began the Gospel, is thus in conformity with God's own view of him. In the depths of his being, Jesus is in unique relationship with God. The plot of the whole gospel narrative revolves around how Jesus lives out this relationship and role, and whether people come to recognise his identity as Messiah, Son of God. Jesus does not linger there by the Jordan; he embarks on his mission without delay.

'Immediately' Jesus is 'driven' into the wilderness by the Spirit. The verb is strong. The purpose for this foray into the Judean desert is to engage Satan in conflict. This encounter and cosmic confrontation is central to the saving plan of God. "He was in the wilderness forty days, tempted by Satan; and he was with the wild beasts; and the angels waited on him." In scripture, the 'wilderness' or 'desert' has different connotations; it is a place of ambiguity. In some contexts, it signifies a privileged place of encounter with God and a place of refuge. Elsewhere, the wilderness is envisaged as the haunt of demons, the theatre of temptation, the domain of evil. Together, the baptism and the testing of Jesus embrace both aspects. So Jesus, under the Spirit's compelling influence, is moving into enemy territory.

---

4 Isa 52:1–53:12.

Mark's storyline is brief. The accounts of the episode in Matthew and Luke are much fuller and more elaborate. They provide dramatic content for the temptations and link them more closely with the Old Testament, the testing of Israel during the forty years of desert wandering and with the 'Son of God' motif. Mark simply states the fact, harsh and unadorned. Mark's most original detail is his comment about the presence of the 'wild beasts'. Instead of the hostility and fear in creation introduced through Satan's victory over Adam, the beasts can be understood as friendly to Jesus. The prophets of old dreamed that when the Messiah came, the wild animals would become tame, live in harmony and not be a threat to human beings, thus restoring the original order of God's creation as it was in the beginning: "they will not hurt or destroy on all my holy mountain".[5] Mark does not specifically say that Jesus is victorious, but an initial victory is implied in the reversal of the effects of the Fall. The evangelist informs us that the "angels" minister to Jesus not just at the end of the forty-day period of trial, as in Matthew and Luke, but throughout the whole time.

So, Mark here provides us with the key to what is to happen in the course of the Gospel, for the mission of Jesus consists in his joining battle with the forces of evil as God's anointed messianic agent. The people of that time viewed physical illness and suffering, psychological problems and moral evil as brought about by demonic forces exerting control over their lives. The vanquishing of Satan, the liberating from his stranglehold, perceived in Jesus' exorcisms and healings, signals the coming of this

---

5 Isa 11:6–9; 35:3–10; 65:24–25; Ezek 34:23–31; Hos 2:18: Ps 91.

new liberation, the inbreak of the Kingdom of God, God's reigning in love.

After the period in the wilderness, the story moves forward, as Jesus decisively embarks on his public mission. Mark writes: "Now after John was arrested, Jesus came to Galilee, proclaiming the good news of God, and saying, 'The time is fulfilled, and the kingdom of God has come near; repent, and believe in the good news'" (1:14-15). The ministry of Jesus begins, and it is carried out not in the Judean desert but as an itinerant, lay prophet in the country villages and by the lakeside of Galilee, and at times further afield. Only at the end of his ministry, as Mark describes it, will he enter Jerusalem.

Preaching or proclaiming is a salient aspect of Jesus' mission. Here, Mark specifies that he announces, "the Good News from God", and then he provides a succinct summary of his message, a kind of manifesto, articulating the heart and essential significance of his whole ministry. Dramatically, Jesus claims that "The time is fulfilled". The lengthy period of hoping and waiting for the liberating and decisive intervention of Israel's God is over. A new phase of history is now beginning, God's appointed moment of opportunity.

The kernel of this gladdening news is that "the Kingdom of God is close at hand", God's reigning presence has arrived. God is now drawing near to His people and His world in love and forgiveness and salvation and is engaged in the overthrowing of the captivity imposed by Satan. The terminology signifies the dynamic exercise of God's sovereignty or dominion, rather than a static territorial area. Throughout his ministry from now on, Jesus will proclaim and make present the kingly rule of God and will enable people to experience it at first hand. The kingdom was clearly Jesus' passion, his dream. The teaching of Jesus was remembered as being characterised by an emphasis on both present and future dimensions of the reigning presence of God.

Central to Jesus' understanding of the Kingdom is the way people respond to the renewed relationship which God is freely offering here and now. With a clear sense of authority, Jesus summons his hearers to a twofold response: repentance and belief, conversion and confidence or trust. The term *metanoia* really means a change of mind, a coming to one's senses, a turning away from sin and back to God, a reorientation of personality, a new way of thinking and valuing and living, a turning round in one's tracks and resuming the right path. Such an about-turn is not simply a personal issue. Jesus' call is for a national conversion—religious, social and political—a returning to genuine loyalty to God at all levels. In this way, God's reign will be restored and more fully established, and evil in its varied forms and dimensions will be displaced and overcome.

Although the element of judgement is contained in this teaching, especially with regard to those who reject God's rule, the salient, characteristic emphasis is placed on salvation. For Jesus, the lordship and sovereignty of God consists in the sovereignty of his love, his ruling in love; God is 'Abba, Father'. The otherness of God, his power and transcendence are manifested in his sovereign freedom to love and to pardon. The coming of the Kingdom is primarily an encounter with the boundless and unmerited mercy of God, the "all inclusive, unconditional love of God, his unreserved acceptance and approval."[6] The Kingdom is gratuitous gift.

So, we know who Jesus is; we have been introduced to the nature of his mission, the establishing of God's reign, which entails the overcoming of evil. And we know the kind of response that he is looking for.

6 Paul Tournier, *Guilt and Grace*, (London: Hodder & Stoughton, 1962), 189.

Chapter Two

The Disciples (Part I)

In Mark's Gospel the two main issues are, first, the identity and role of Jesus and secondly, the nature of discipleship. Discipleship is a fascinating theme. It runs through the whole narrative like a thread, and so it can serve as a kind of skeleton or outline for the whole gospel story. At one level it deals with the historic disciples of Jesus; at another it was addressed to the Christian community of Mark's day, and at yet another level it speaks to us today, as we identify with them in their struggle to come to terms with what it means in practice to follow Jesus.

The first public act of Jesus' ministry, in fact, is to call four people (two pairs) to follow him, to be his disciples. Jesus is walking along by the inland lake usually referred to as the Sea of Galilee. The excellent fish supplies supported a thriving fishing industry with an export market, acknowledged in secular literature of the period. Throughout Mark's Gospel there is always a sense of movement about Jesus, a breathless urgency almost. Mark frequently uses the word 'immediately'. The two brief call episodes are told in parallel in a stylised manner (1:16–20). They follow a scheme devoid of biographical detail, a scheme calculated to highlight points of wider Christian theological interest.

Jesus "sees" the individuals concerned. They are busy about their normal daily tasks. Simon and Andrew, as they are named, are "at work with a casting-net". It is in the midst of their ordinary routine existence that Jesus breaks into their lives. No mention is made of any particular qualities or aptitudes. It is Jesus who takes the initiative; he freely chooses and calls. Normally, a rabbi waited for would-be disciples to come to him and 'sign on', as it were, in his school with a view to studying the Law. With Jesus the reverse is the case. Jesus speaks his authoritative "Follow me". His word lays hold on their lives. Jesus isn't asking them to become temporary students, but to be with him, to enter into a lifelong personal relationship, to share his life. He continues: "I will make you into fishers of people". This implies that all that will become of the disciples will take place because of the initiative of Jesus and their association with him. Their call to discipleship is also a call to ministry, to share the mission of Jesus, to follow him and engage in his task of winning (netting) people for the Kingdom. The two respond immediately, decisively and unconditionally. The authority and personality of Jesus are such that at this first meeting, they leave their nets, their means of employment, livelihood and security, and follow him.

In the parallel story, James, son of Zebedee, and his brother John are in their boat mending their nets. Again, Jesus is walking by; he "sees" them and calls them "immediately", and they leave their father and hired men behind in the boat. There is a touch of poignancy about the wording. Now, Zebedee is dependent on hired men rather than on his sons. There is a radical aspect to the following of Jesus. It entails a willingness to break with the past, to leave livelihood and what is familiar and even to sever natural personal ties. Such an abrupt departure would have been a shock to the cultural values of the time.

The same format is repeated a little later in the calling of Levi (2:14). Jesus is again by the lake, teaching the crowds who have gathered there. He then "walks along" and "sees" Levi, son of Alphaeus, at his daily work, "sitting at the tax booth". Jesus pronounces his authoritative summons "Follow me"; Levi jumps up and follows. Whereas the earlier disciples were self-employed fishermen and could have returned to their work, Levi, having resigned from Herod's tax administration, may not have been able to get his job back. Technically, Levi was a customs officer in the service of Herod, a Jewish client king (or tetrarch) appointed by Rome. But Levi is a man despised, a sinner in the popular estimation, outside the community of Judaism. Such men had a reputation for dishonesty and extortion; they also mixed with non-Jews. The freedom, originality and generosity of Jesus are startlingly evident as he cuts through conventional barriers and reaches out to those on the margins of religion, an outreach which upsets the religious elite. It was scandalous that he should include such a person in his circle. This is continued in the subsequent scene when Jesus shares a meal with "tax collectors and sinners". There is no mention of their conversion, repentance or restitution. Jesus is at home with them. Such table fellowship becomes a key aspect of Jesus' outreach to others.

A little later in the narrative, there is another version of the calling of the disciples, which I find quite moving, and which sums up Mark's understanding of the nature of discipleship (now as then). The impression conveyed is that there were many people around Jesus. After being rejected by the religious and civil authorities after curing the man with the withered arm (3:6), Jesus decides to choose from this wider group a small, symbolic band of twelve who will be the nucleus of the new Israel, the new people of God. The wording is significant. Jesus "singled out" or "summoned" those whom "he wanted". Again, the initiative lies totally with him, with his gracious freedom. Those chosen respond: "they came away to him". Jesus appoints or designates twelve. They are "to be with" him, to share his intimacy and friendship, to share his life, to come to share his outlook, vision, understanding and ideals. A deep personal relationship is established. And secondly, they are "to be sent", to share his mission. And the mission is articulated in two spheres: to proclaim the gospel, to share with others the Good News; and secondly, to drive out devils, to combat evil in all its forms, which is the negative way of talking about the establishing of God's reign. So, the mission of the disciples is couched in the same terms as the mission of Jesus. It is a very synthetic but powerful presentation of the nature of Christian discipleship. And that applies to each one of us too. We are called "to be with" and "to be sent", relationship and mission in tandem. And then Mark lists the familiar names, adding to the name of Judas, "who betrayed him" (3:13–19). From this point on, I will focus on this group of twelve, aware that there are other followers of Jesus beyond them, not least the women who "used to follow him and provided for him when in Galilee" (15:40).

In the next lengthy block of material (4:1–6:6), Mark emphasises the aspect of *being with* Jesus. In chapter 4 the disciples are with Jesus as he seeks to explain the nature of the Kingdom through his teaching, his proclaiming, his preaching in parables. Here, the evangelist gathers together a number of the parables of Jesus to form a block, a unit. The gospels of Matthew and Luke contain far more parables than that of Mark. Here in Mark we find the parable of the sower (4:3–9) and its explanation (4:14–20); the lamp under a basket (4:21–25); the growing seed, a parable only in Mark (4:26–29); and the mustard seed (4:30–32). For our theme, two points are worth noting. First, Jesus goes out of his way to explain the parables to the disciples. "To you has been given the secret of the kingdom of God..." (4:11); "but he explained everything in private to his disciples" (4:34). It is part of the "being with", and a preparation for the "being sent". Secondly, the disciples obviously have problems in seeing, in understanding; they are slow on the uptake. "Do you not understand this parable?" asks Jesus, "Then how will you understand all the parables?" The theme of the disciples' failure is introduced.

The story moves quickly on, and the disciples are "with him" as he performs a series of remarkable miracles. Mark prefers to call these 'mighty works'. There is the calming of the storm (4:35–41), the dramatic exorcism of the wild man ('Legion') in the country of the Gerasenes (5:1–17), the healing of the woman with the haemorrhage problem (5:25–34), and the raising to life of Jairus' daughter (5:21–24, 35–43). Each episode illustrates in different ways the authority and kindness of Jesus and is evidence that through him the Kingdom of God is breaking in; it is not simply a nice idea but a reality which can be experienced.

In the first of these stories the disciples receive a reprimand from Jesus for being cowardly and lacking in faith, as they panic in the midst of the storm which has suddenly arisen, and awaken Jesus, as he sleeps in the stern of the boat. "Why are you afraid? Have you still no faith?" On the positive side, they ask one another the right question: "Who then is this, that even the wind and the sea obey him?" There is also an interesting conclusion to the exorcism of Legion, for, as Jesus goes along with the request of the local people that he should leave their neighbourhood, the formerly possessed man begs Jesus to be allowed to go "with him". This Jesus will not permit; he is the one who does the choosing. However, he tells him: "Go home to your friends, and tell them how much the Lord has done for you, and what mercy he has shown you" (5:19). And the man sets off and proclaims in that predominantly Gentile region what Jesus has done for him. He is the precursor of the post-resurrection mission to the Gentiles. In the story of the raising to life of the daughter of Jairus, a sequence which illustrates Mark's 'sandwich' technique, an interesting feature is Jesus' selection of three of his disciples to accompany him: Peter, James and John. They will be present also at the Transfiguration and in Gethsemane. They seem to form an inner circle.

After this series of mighty works, Jesus goes to his hometown of Nazareth (6:1–6), accompanied by his disciples, and preaches in the synagogue on the Sabbath. Initially, the response is positive; the people are in awe at his wisdom and deeds of power. They wonder where he gets it all from. But their acquaintance with his ordinary background as a craftsman and with his family members leads them to be suspicious and even hostile. In 'small-town resentment' they turn against him and his message, and reject him, a presage of wider rejection which is to follow. Jesus is "amazed at their unbelief". The disciples must have been taken aback at what happened. It was a sad experience to share, but a valuable lesson for their formation. Jesus leaves the place and does not return.

Having "been with" Jesus for a while, and been present for his teaching and mighty works, the twin aspects of his mission, the disciples are then sent out on mission themselves in twos according to Jewish custom. The text says that "they went out and proclaimed that all should repent. They cast out many demons, and anointed with oil many who were sick and cured them" (6:12). In fact, their ministry is one of both word and deed, but they preach a preparatory repentance rather than the presence of the Kingdom. It is clear that their authority depends on close association with Jesus. In their absence, Mark records the death of the Baptist. It serves as a kind of narrative interlude (6:14–29).

On returning from their expedition, the disciples, here referred to as "apostles" for the only time in Mark, report to Jesus "all that they had done and taught", again specifying both aspects of mission. It is so very human. They just have to tell Jesus everything. I wonder, however, whether there is a hint of trouble ahead in that they speak of what "they" have done and taught. It seems as if they have understood their activity and success as independent of Jesus. Their leaving and returning form a frame for the story of the death of John the Baptist. This framing technique occurs several times in the Markan narrative. John's murder is a sobering reminder of the element of suffering—an element shortly to be further developed explicitly.

As Jesus listens to their various accounts of what has happened, he realises that they need a break—a very sensitive, understanding touch. "Come with me, by yourselves, to some lonely place where you can rest quietly". The attempt to get away fails, as people come to hear of their departure, and are waiting for them when their boat reaches the destination. Jesus is moved to compassion at the sight of the crowds, "because they were like sheep without a shepherd", and he taught them at great length and then provided them with something to eat—the story of the multiplication of the loaves and fishes; again, word and action combined (6:35–44).

In the next section of the Gospel, Mark structures his narrative in a carefully crafted and interesting way. We find two sequences which unfold in parallel. The first sequence consists of five elements: the feeding of the 5000 (6:35–44), the crossing of the lake when Jesus walks on the water (6:45–52), a controversy with the Pharisees (7:1–23), a story which contains a reference to bread (7:24–30—the Syrophoenician woman), and a story of the healing of a deaf mute (7:31–37). The parallel sequence which follows offers us the feeding of the 4000 (8:1–9), a reference to the crossing of the lake (8:10), a brief controversy (8:11–13), a discussion about bread as they again cross the lake (8:14–21), and the healing of a blind man (8:22–26). The two healing miracles which conclude each section are found only in Mark, and recall Isaiah 35:5: "Then the eyes of the blind will be opened and the ears of the deaf unstopped".

For our theme of discipleship there are several telling comments in the course of these two structurally parallel sections. Forming the prelude to the feeding of the 5000 narrative, it is the disciples who approach Jesus, actually suggesting that he should send the people away so that they can find food for themselves. They are then disconcerted when Jesus intimates that they should provide the food themselves (6:36–37). Then, after Jesus has multiplied the loaves and fishes, sent the crowds away and enjoined that they set out across the lake again, they are overcome with terror at the sight of him, as he comes to join them, walking on the water. Mark comments: "At this they were completely dumbfounded, for they had not understood the incident of the loaves: their minds were closed" (6:52). They have problems understanding the words of Jesus in his subsequent controversy with the religious leaders about ritual defilement, which prompts Jesus to ask: "Do you also fail to understand?" (7:18).

Later, in the second sequence of events, when the crowds gather again and have nothing to eat, the compassion of Jesus and his desire that they be fed receives the following reply from his disciples: "How can one feed these people with bread here in the desert?" They have short memories! Jesus uses the seven loaves which they have brought with them to feed the 4000. After this second multiplication of the loaves, the Pharisees ask Jesus for a sign from heaven; they are unwilling to accept the signs he has given (8:11–13). So, Jesus and the twelve cross the lake again, and the disciples become worried because they have forgotten to bring with them adequate bread supplies; they have only one loaf. Jesus has to administer a trenchant rebuke: "Why are you talking about having no bread? Do you still not perceive or understand? Are your hearts hardened? Do you have eyes and fail to see? Do you have ears and fail to hear? Do you not yet understand?" (8:17–21). The disciples are blind; they desperately need Jesus to lead them into understanding and bring them to sight.

Chapter Three

The Disciples (Part II)

The next episode is a fascinating story (8:22–26). Structurally, it looks both ways; it serves as a bridge passage. It brings the second five-item sequence to a conclusion and is in parallel with the conclusion of the first sequence, the cure of the deaf mute. Together these cures fulfil the prophecy of Isaiah, as we saw. It also introduces the next main section of Mark's story, sometimes called 'the journey narrative', which is framed by two incidents in which Jesus cures a blind man ('from blind to blind'). It serves as a paradigm, a model, for Jesus' dealings with the disciples in the remainder of the gospel, as he seeks to lead them from blindness to understanding and the insight of faith. The second half of the Gospel begins here.

This first story involving a blind man is often referred to as a two-stage miracle. It is the only miracle story in the Gospels in which Jesus is not immediately successful. It is symbolic of the gradual process of the disciples moving into faith; until the resurrection, they remain only half-seeing. The story is to be understood in conjunction with the following incident at Caesarea Philippi; they are cleverly paired. The setting is Bethsaida. Some people bring a blind man to Jesus, asking that he "touch" him. In doing so, they show faith in Jesus. It is assumed that contact with Jesus is curative. Jesus takes the man by the hand and leads him outside the village away from the others, probably to avoid a public spectacle. He spits into his eyes and lays his hands on him. In the earlier parallel story Jesus spits on his own fingers and touches the man's tongue with his moistened fingers. Here, Jesus then asks whether he can see anything. The man is beginning to see, but still cannot distinguish objects too well; his vision is blurred. He replies: "I can see people, but they look like trees, walking." Perhaps he is peering into the distance to see his friends, since Jesus has led him away from them. Jesus then touches the man's eyes again without using spittle, and he comes to complete sight. "He looked intently and his sight was restored, and he saw everything clearly." Thus, the man makes a journey from no sight through partial vision to full sight. Jesus sends him home.

The story is very significant for Mark. It is placed immediately after the blindness of the disciples has been rigorously and emphatically highlighted, their need to be led into sight and understanding. The story is symbolic of coming to faith. It illustrates this possibility. It sets the scene for the section 8:27–10:52, and for the rest of the Gospel. The disciples will not finally see clearly until after Jesus' death and resurrection. The parallel with the next incident at Caesarea Philippi is deliberate.

Within the 'blind to blind' framework for the next three chapters is to be found a pattern which consists of Jesus three times predicting his suffering, death and subsequent vindication. Each prediction is followed by an indication that the disciples fail to understand and accept, for they cannot yet see. Jesus responds by imparting some clear teaching on the nature of discipleship.

Jesus and the disciples are on the move again, journeying north to the villages or small settlements near Caesarea Philippi, which was situated at a source of the Jordan on the lower southern slopes of Mount Hermon, some twenty-five miles from Bethsaida. Jesus takes the initiative in questioning the disciples concerning people's opinions and views about himself. His question is: "Who do people say that I am?" (8:27). The identity of Jesus is a central theme of the Gospel. This question has been lurking behind the narrative since 1:14.

Their reply suggests that on the part of the common folk generally, Jesus was recognised as a prophet, since he claimed to speak for God. Some think that he might be John the Baptist, others Elijah, others one of the prophets of old. Jesus probes further, challenging the disciples about their own estimation of him: "But who do you say that I am?" The "you" is emphatic. Peter, as spokesman, boldly professes his belief that Jesus is the "Messiah". It seems that at last the truth is dawning. But we know from the introduction (1:1; 1:11) that Jesus is also Son of God, and this does not get a mention. Peter's statement is correct, but there is more. He sees, but not clearly; he is correct, but only partially. Jesus neither endorses nor rejects Peter's response but imposes silence. To broadcast the idea that he was messiah would have been dangerous, because the common expectation was that the messiah would accomplish his work through the exercise of power and would be a manifestly glorious and victorious military figure. This conflicts with Jesus' own understanding of his mission.

This is the turning point of the Gospel, the hinge, pivot, watershed, as an answer is given to the question of Jesus' messianic identity just proclaimed by Peter. The dominant theme is now that of the cross. Jesus responds to Peter's confession by speaking openly about his identity and destiny for the first time, the nature of his messiahship. His beginning to teach suggests a new orientation. "Then he began to teach them that the Son of Man must undergo great suffering, and be rejected by the elders, the chief priests and the scribes, and be killed, and after three days rise again" (8:31). The word "must" is emphatic and acknowledges that what will inevitably happen is part of God's plan, and is an event of eschatological significance, not just an unavoidable tragedy. Historically, the simplest form of the prediction was probably "the Son of Man must suffer many things". The formulation of the rest owes a great deal to the story of what in fact happened; this has been read back into Jesus' life. Jesus must also have expressed confidence in his subsequent vindication in some form or other, perhaps with less precision than is stated here; the reference to resurrection may reflect later Christian experience of the way in which that vindication occurred.

Jesus' words must have come as a shock; they provoke a bewildered and vehement protest from Peter. Clearly, he has only partial vision; he cannot accept this new idea about suffering and death; it does not fit in with his expectations or his appreciation of Jesus' mission; he has not grasped the essential meaning of messiahship. There are, of course, implications here for his own discipleship; following a suffering messiah is not what he was anticipating; it is hardly an attractive option. Jesus then turns and looks at his disciples; they, too, are included in what follows. He then publicly "rebukes" Peter in strong terms for his repudiation of the way of suffering, for his thinking as men think rather than as God thinks. Jesus says: "Get behind me, Satan." This suggests that Peter is playing Satan's role in tempting Jesus, seeking to persuade him to adopt a different form of messiahship and attempting to block his way.

Jesus rather abruptly summons the crowd along with the disciples, for everyone needs to know his message about discipleship, (including the reader). He then spells out the nature of discipleship openly and unequivocally. There is a series of statements: "If any want to become my followers, let them deny themselves and take up their cross and follow me". A disciple must walk in the suffering path of Jesus. Loyalty and faithfulness are called for; here it means being no longer preoccupied with self, personal interests and desires, self-fulfilment, but to have Jesus in the centre (8:34–38).

Jesus now refers to his passion for the second time, and the disciples fail to understand what he was saying and "were afraid to ask him" (9:30–32). As the journey continues towards Capernaum, the disciples argue with one another about seniority, importance and greatness. When they reach their destination and are in the house, Jesus challenges them about this. There is an embarrassed silence. Jesus states: "whoever wants to be first must be last of all and servant of all". The emphasis switches from suffering and cross-bearing to humility and service. Jesus illustrates his meaning by taking a little child in his arms. Rather than quarrelling about greatness and control, they should be open and receptive like a child; they ought also to be concerned with the weak members of the community (9:33–37).

As the journey continues there is important teaching about different aspects of discipleship. In response to a question from the Pharisees, Jesus outlines his view about divorce, and clarifies this to the disciples later in the house when they question him further (10:2–12). People then bring little children to Jesus so that he might touch them in blessing. The disciples speak sternly to them, seeking to deter them. Jesus is annoyed by this, and states: "Let the little children come to me; do not stop them; for it is to such as these that the kingdom of God belongs". Jesus takes them in his arms and blesses them (10:13–16). Next, the issue of riches and possessions is raised. After the prospective disciple has gone away from Jesus shocked and downcast when told that discipleship for him entailed the giving up of his possessions, Jesus comments on the difficulty rich people will have to enter God's Kingdom. Since this idea contradicts popular biblical wisdom, the disciples are perplexed and astounded. Peter then speaks up once again: "Look, we have left everything and followed you." Jesus promises them a hundredfold in this life—along with persecutions, and eternal life in the age to come (10:28–31).

Mark then describes the disciples on the road going to Jerusalem, with Jesus walking determinedly ahead. They are amazed and afraid. Jesus takes the twelve aside and tells them once more about what is to befall him. Their failure to understand and accept is illustrated by the next incident, in which the two sons of Zebedee make a bid for the top jobs in the coming Kingdom. The rest, when they get to hear about this, are naturally very indignant.

Jesus again attempts to open their eyes and minds to the nature of his messiahship and the Kingdom, and to the real meaning of discipleship: "You know that among the Gentiles those whom they recognise as their rulers lord it over them, and their great ones are tyrants over them. But it is not so among you. Whoever wishes to be great among you must be your servant, and whoever wishes to be first among you must be slave of all. For the Son of Man came not to be served but to serve, and to give his life as a ransom for many" (10:35–45). The messianic way of Jesus is the way of self-giving service, a way which turns the way of contemporary culture ("the way men think") on its head.

Jesus and his disciples reach the garden city of Jericho. As they set off for the final leg of their journey to Jerusalem, he gives sight to Bartimaeus, the episode which brings this section of the Gospel to a close. This is the last of Jesus' cures, and is to be taken in conjunction with the earlier story of the two-stage cure of the blind man outside his village. The two stories, as we have noted, frame the section in which Jesus has been attempting to open the eyes of the disciples. The blind man, sitting begging by the roadside, shouts out, asking Jesus to have pity on him. People, maybe including the disciples, insensitively tell him to be quiet. But Jesus stops, calls him over, asks what he wants and cures him. The story ends: "he regained his sight and followed Jesus on the way" (10:46–52).

Mark's story of Jesus has gradually but clearly been moving to its Calvary climax. Mark's passion narrative is excellently crafted, beginning with the Passover meal. Mark's structure of the meal is powerful. With simplicity and economy, it contains three episodes, two at the Supper itself, and a third as Jesus and his disciples leave the supper room for the Mount of Olives. First, Jesus speaks about the coming betrayal to be perpetrated by one of the twelve, a friend and table companion, who partakes of the same dish (14:17–21; see Ps 41:9). Secondly, he then speaks words over the bread and cup; this is Mark's main focus (14:22–25). And thirdly, as they leave the supper room after the meal and concluding psalms, Jesus, in shepherding language recalling Zechariah (13:7), foretells the scattering and flight of all the disciples and the denials of Peter (14:26–31).

But in the tragedy of it all there is a note of hope as he promises that he will later go before them into Galilee. The two pointers to the inadequacy and failure of the disciples, his close friends, chosen to be "with him" (3:14), serves as the framework for the Eucharistic words and action of Jesus, which express his deep, self-giving love. This structural shape highlights the significance of the central event and the contrast between Jesus and his disciples. It also shows that Mark's agenda, as throughout his Gospel, includes both the self-giving of Jesus and the failure of his disciples.

The discipleship theme, then, provides us with an overview of the whole Gospel narrative. It provides a wonderful definition of discipleship for us: be with and be sent. It illustrates the struggles and challenges of discipleship and highlights a lifestyle of self-giving and service.

Chapter Four

The Little People

The 'little people' is a name I like to use to describe the minor characters in Mark's story. They do not really form a group but are a collection of individuals who have a single encounter with Jesus and then move off stage. But they are very significant players in the Gospel drama because they help us to appreciate the freedom and compassion of Jesus, and they illustrate the qualities of genuine discipleship. For convenience, I will discuss them under three heading: First, there are a number of people who show great faith in seeking help for others; secondly, there are several individuals who also show great faith, but this time in seeking healing for themselves rather than for others; and thirdly, there are those who manifest qualities of service and generosity.

Early in the narrative there is the wonderful story of a group of friends who bring to Jesus a man who is paralysed. Because of the crowds, they cannot get access to the house where Jesus is teaching, so they climb onto the flat roof and lower the invalid down through the roof—the original drop-in centre. They are obviously really good, helpful friends and go to remarkable lengths to get him to Jesus. Jesus recognises their great faith, too, and responds by initially forgiving the paralysed man, and then he tells him to "stand up and take your mat and walk". This he does, for he is cured and restored to his family and to normal life (2:1–12).

Later, there is a synagogue ruler named Jairus, one of the very few people whose name we get to know. In great distress, he approaches Jesus, falls at his feet, and asks him to come and heal his daughter, who is on the point of death. Whilst on their way to his house, news comes that the girl has died, there is no point in troubling Jesus further; it is too late. Jesus, however, tells Jairus to carry on believing. They reach the house, where there is a great commotion and loud weeping. Jesus enters their house, and says to the child "Little girl, get up", and she does, and begins to walk around. To her parents, who are amazed, Jesus suggests that they should give her something to eat—such a human touch (5:35–43).

The next episode occurs after the feeding of the 5000 and the subsequent altercation with the Pharisees and scribes about ritual defilement. Jesus moves away to the predominantly Gentile region of Tyre, seeking to be alone for a while. A woman who hails from Syro-Phoenicia, clearly a Gentile, finds out that Jesus is in town and approaches him with the request that he heal her daughter who is afflicted with a devil. Initially, Jesus is hesitant, since he understands his mission at that stage to be primarily directed to his own people. But her faith and clever repartee win the day, and she gets her wish. Returning home, she finds her daughter "lying on the bed, and the demon gone" (7:24–30).

Shortly after this, probably still on Gentile soil, some people bring to Jesus a deaf man who also has a speech impediment, and they beg Jesus to "lay his hand on him". Jesus takes him away from the crowd, touches his ears and tongue, looks up to heaven and sighs "Be opened". The man finds that he is now able to hear and to speak clearly (7:31–37). A little later, there is the story told in parallel in which, having returned to Bethsaida, Jesus is approached by some people bringing with them a blind man, with the request that he touch him. Again, Jesus takes him to one side, touches his eyes with saliva and lays his hands on him. The man begins to see, but not clearly. Jesus lays hands on him again, "and his sight was restored, and he saw everything clearly" (8:22–26).

Finally in this series, there is the man whose son is suffering from chronic epilepsy. In Jesus' absence on the mountain of transfiguration, the disciples fail in their attempts to help him. When Jesus reaches the group, the man turns to him, providing a vivid description of the young man's affliction. The father says: "If you are able to do anything, have compassion on us and help us." Jesus challenges the quality of his faith, to which he makes that wonderful confession: "I do believe; help my unbelief." Jesus then orders the unclean spirit to come out of him, which it does, throwing the boy to the ground in a convulsion. Jesus then takes him by the hand and lifts him up to new life (9:14–29).

The second group of individuals also show great faith, but this time in seeking healing for themselves rather than for others. Very early in the story there is the leper who approaches Jesus seeking to be cleansed. His disease entailed segregation from the social and religious life of the community. His life was thus a misery, a source of physical discomfort, mental anguish and also spiritual guilt, because leprosy was deemed to be evidence of and punishment for sin; a leper was considered unclean in the religious sense too. The man has real faith that Jesus can do so, but is not sure that he will, given that he is himself breaking the Law in approaching him, and Jesus would be infringing regulations in coming into contact with him. "If you want to, you can make me clean." Jesus replies compassionately: "Of course I want to." And Jesus actually touches the untouchable as an expression of his compassion, ignoring the risk of contagion and incurring the stigma of ritual defilement according to the Law. He makes him clean, liberates him from his isolation, restoring him to the normal life of his community, and enables him to experience the dawning Kingdom, the presence of a gracious God (1:40–45).

Another moving episode occurs within the structural frame created by the two phases of the story of Jairus: his initial approach to Jesus, then his going to his house with Jesus and his three companions after his daughter's death. There is a large crowd around Jesus, amongst them a woman suffering from a serious menstrual problem for twelve years. She seems to have done the rounds of the medical profession to no avail, and this has drained her financial resources. Such a condition rendered her ritually unclean, which entailed isolation and guilt. She decides to seek healing, and comes up behind Jesus in the crowd, believing that touching his cloak would be enough. It was; she is cured. But then Jesus will not allow her to melt back into the crowd. Aware that someone has touched him, he wishes to meet the person face to face. She comes forward, falls at his feet and explains her situation. A relationship is established, and Jesus addresses her warmly: "Your faith has made you well; go in peace, and be healed of your disease" (5:25–34).

In an earlier chapter we met blind Bartimaeus begging outside the city of Jericho on the pilgrimage route. On hearing that Jesus is passing by, he shouts out "Jesus, Son of David, have mercy on me." Many of the pilgrims tell him to be quiet, but he calls out all the more insistently. Jesus stops, and calls him to him. Jesus then asks that poignant question: "What do you want me to do for you?" Bartimaeus begs to be able to see again. Jesus tells him to go, for "your faith has made you well." But Bartimaeus does not go; now that he can see, he joins Jesus, following him "on the way" (10:46–52).

The third group in our sequence of minor characters are people who show generosity and a spirit of service First, there is Simon's mother-in-law, very early in the story, who, when Jesus cures her of her fever, immediately sets about preparing a meal for him and for the others (1:30–31). During Jesus' final week in Jerusalem, there are two other women who show remarkable generosity. Jesus and his disciples are sitting opposite the treasury in the temple, watching folk making their donations. Many of the pilgrims are wealthy and contribute large sums. A widow comes along and puts into the money box two small copper coins, financially worthless. Jesus is quick to draw the attention of the disciples to this, pointing out that her contribution is worth more than the large amounts offered by the wealthy, for she has put in "all she had to live on." She kept nothing back (12:41–44).

Later that week, Jesus is a guest at a meal in the house of a former leper called Simon. An unnamed woman enters with an alabaster jar of very costly ointment. She breaks the jar open and pours the contents on his head; there is nothing left. Others present are critical of her action, considering it a waste and suggesting that it would have been better to sell it and give the money to the poor. But Jesus defends her: "Let her alone. She has performed a good service for me." He adds: "She has done what she could; she has anointed my body beforehand for its burial." He intimates that she will be remembered wherever in the world the Good News will be preached; and she is (14:3–9).

These two women are remembered for their generosity, their holding nothing back in their love and service; they give everything. Their unselfish generosity is a prelude to Jesus himself giving everything a few days later on Calvary.

This catalogue of episodes in which Jesus encounters the 'little people' is informative and very beautiful, highlighting central aspects of discipleship in such a positive and inspiring manner. Jesus himself comes across as extremely kind and compassionate, but also as remarkably free, as in many cases he breaks the rules in order to reach out to serve and help. The two concluding stories open the way to our final chapter, the death and resurrection of Jesus.

Chapter Five

The Opposition

The next group of people I wish to consider can be referred to as 'the opposition'. In the main, those who oppose Jesus throughout his ministry, attempt to make life difficult for him and, finally, seek to get rid of him are the scribes, the Pharisees and the Jerusalem priestly aristocracy. At the end of the story, the Romans get involved and Herod, their appointee as tetrarch, also gets mentioned. Historically, he was a dangerous figure, a problematic constant in the background.

The Pharisees, or 'separated ones', were a dynamic and very influential group. They had no particular membership requirements except a serious commitment to the Law and a lively concern to apply it to their daily lives. They advocated the study of scripture. They were unhappy with the situation in the temple and the lack of observance of purity there.[1] They believed passionately in the oral Torah and the ancient traditions of interpretation handed down

1 Francis J. Moloney, *Reading the New Testament in the Church*, (Grand Rapids, MI; Baker Academic, 2015), 31.

over centuries ('the traditions of the elders'). Within them was a group called *haberim*, like a guild of friends or associates, who were very strict and who pledged to keep the Law with precision. Some advocated adherence in daily life to the purity regulations practised by the priests in the temple. Because they were laymen and free from temple and priestly commitments, they were able to reach out pastorally to Jews who lived in the diaspora far from Jerusalem. There they established synagogues. The negative portrayal of them in the Gospels reflects something of the tension between rabbinic Judaism and the early Church after the destruction of the temple and city in 70CE.

Frequently, the Pharisees are associated with the scribes. Many, but not all, were scribes. The scribes were not a specific religious group but were the legal experts of Israel, the professional scholars, the rabbis. They were the religious leaders, respected and influential. They also served as lawyers.

Another important group were the Sadducees. The Sadducees (the name probably derives from the high priest Zadok in Solomon's time) were probably the most powerful Jewish group of Jesus' day. They were wealthy, based in Jerusalem and many were priests; they controlled the temple system, with its sacrifices and forms of worship, and they often dominated the Sanhedrin, the main legislative body. They had close links with the priestly aristocracy, many of whom were themselves Sadducees, probably including the high priest. They were theologically a rather conservative group. They did not believe in angels, the resurrection or the afterlife; they regarded only the Pentateuch as sacred scripture and did not accept the oral traditions. They did not support armed struggle and tended to cooperate with Rome in a way which enabled them to preserve the status quo. They were the main architects of the plot to exterminate Jesus. Any influence they had faded with the destruction of the temple.

In Jerusalem there were the high priest, members of the priestly families and the lay aristocracy. These were the real power brokers in Israel, and usually quite wealthy. The High Priest was a Roman appointee. The priests obviously had a key role in daily temple worship and for the key pilgrimage feasts of Passover, Tabernacles and Pentecost. The Herodians, mentioned twice in Mark's Gospel, were political supporters of Herod the tetrarch.

The way Mark handles the issue of opposition to Jesus is to present the reader with two main blocks of material, usually referred to as controversy stories. The first is found early in the narrative (chapter 2 and the beginning of 3); the second during Jesus' final week in Jerusalem (chapters 11 and 12). But in reality, Jesus' whole ministry was punctuated with controversy; several incidents at different points throughout the story remind us of this.

Let us briefly examine the first block. We should not think that Jesus has a really bad day, moving from one problem or crisis to another. No! Mark has brought together in a literary unit several controversies which would have occurred at different times and in different places. The setting for the first controversy is the healing of the paralysed man, or rather, the fact that as well as curing the man, Jesus forgives his sins. The scribes are unhappy with this, as only God can forgive, so they believe that Jesus is blaspheming, a serious charge. But the Son of Man, says Jesus, has authority on earth to forgive sins (2:1–12).

The second issue which occurs is the fact that, at the party which Levi throws after being called by Jesus, the guests include people whom the religious elite considered to be 'sinners'. Again, it is the scribes, who here are also Pharisees, who complain, asking why Jesus is sharing table in this way. He replies with a touch of irony that a doctor's role is to attend to the sick, not to those who think they are healthy. He has come "to call not the righteous, but sinners" (2:13–17). The third problem to arise stems from the fact that the Pharisees and also the disciples of the Baptist used to fast regularly, whereas Jesus and his disciples did not. Jesus is asked to provide an explanation. His reply is a little enigmatic: wedding guests do not fast when the bridegroom is with them. However, they will fast after the bridegroom has been taken away, after his death. The 'bridegroom' was a messianic image, so Jesus is inviting his critics to open their eyes and see that something special is happening here (2:18–20).

The fourth problem has to do with Sabbath observance, which was a very important facet of Jewish religious living. The disciples of Jesus are plucking heads of grain as they walk through the cornfields on the Sabbath. This time it is the Pharisees who are critical of this behaviour. Jesus reminds them of what David did, and makes that amazing statement: "The Sabbath was made for humankind, and not humankind for the Sabbath; so the Son of Man is lord even of the Sabbath." "Son of Man" is the term Jesus often used when speaking of himself (2:23–28). Finally, Jesus is in the synagogue on another Sabbath, and there is a man present with a withered hand. The Pharisees are watching him to see whether he will cure on the Sabbath, which they considered to be against the Law. They are out to get him here; some scholars wonder whether the man was a 'plant'. Jesus calls the man out into the middle of the assembly and asks whether on the Sabbath one should do good or harm. The Pharisees refuse to answer. He is annoyed with them, "grieved at their hardness of heart". He provides an answer to his own question by curing the man, by opting for goodness. At this, the Pharisees go out and join up with the supporters of Herod, an odd liaison; the two conspire "how to destroy him". From now on, as Mark's story unfolds, Jesus lives under the shadow of the cross (3:1–6).

The story moves on. Soon afterwards, the scribes come down from the city of Jerusalem and accuse Jesus of casting out devils through the power of Satan (3:22–30). Basically, they are saying that he himself is devil-possessed, a very hostile accusation. Jesus turns the tables on them by commenting that a kingdom divided against itself cannot stand; their criticism clearly makes no sense. He adds a further comment, that no one can enter a strong man's house and plunder his property without first tying up the strong man. Clearly, Jesus is the stronger one (an echo of 1:7). Later, after the feeding of the 5000, some Pharisees and some Jerusalem scribes approach Jesus. Noticing that Jesus' disciples failed to wash their hands before eating, they ask Jesus why his disciples do not live according to the traditions of the elders. Jesus quotes the prophet Isaiah to them: they honour God with their lips, but their hearts are far from Him. He goes on to teach that defilement does not derive from outside a person, but from what is within our human hearts. This is a stringent critique of purification rites (7:1–23). Later, after the feeding of the 4000, some Pharisees come up and argue with him, demanding a sign from heaven to authenticate his ministry. Jesus refuses, because he has already given so many signs that he comes from God, and they are not prepared to recognise this (8:11–13).

The next block of controversies is located in the final week of Jesus' life after he has entered Jerusalem on what we now call Palm Sunday, though there are no palms in Mark's description of the event (11:1–11). On the following day, Jesus enters the temple and drives out those buying and selling, overturning the tables of the money lenders, a dramatic prophet gesture. The day after that, as he is walking in the temple again, he is challenged by the chief priests, scribes and elders—the real power brokers—asking where he gets the authority to do these things. In reply, he asks them a question: whether John's baptism came from men or from God—a very clever question which puts them on the spot, since they had not believed John, and the people considered him a prophet. They refuse to give an answer, so Jesus, too, refuses (11:27–33).

He then tells a parable in which the owner of a vineyard leases it out to tenants. At the time of the harvest he sends his slave to get the produce, but the tenants beat him up; the same happens to the next one he sends; a third envoy is murdered. Finally, he sends his son, confident that they will respect him. But the tenants decide to kill him so that they will inherit the vineyard. The religious leaders realise that this parable is aimed at them; they want to arrest Jesus, but are afraid of the crowd, so they make their exit (12:1–12). The Pharisees and Herodians join together next, asking whether or not it is lawful to pay taxes to Caesar, a question intended to place Jesus in a no-win situation and discredit him. Jesus is well aware of their ploy, and he outwits them by asking whose head is on the coin. They acknowledge that it the Emperor's. Jesus comments that they should give to Caesar what is Caesar's, then, but he challengingly adds that they should also give to God what is God's (12:13–17).

Now it is the turn of the Sadducees. This group did not believe in the resurrection and seek to ridicule the idea. Jesus tells them that they have got it wrong, they don't understand the scriptures or what resurrection is about (12:27). One of the scribes then asks him about the greatest commandment. In Mark this is a genuine question, not a test, as in Matthew. Jesus and the scribe agree on this point: the greatest commandment is to love God with one's whole being, but also, Jesus adds, to love one's neighbour as oneself. Jesus tells him that he is not far from the Kingdom of God (12:28–32). Then Jesus himself goes onto the attack, denouncing the scribes for always wanting to be greeted with respect, grabbing the best seats in the synagogues, the places of honour at banquets, saying long prayers just for show (12:38–40).

Mark then states that two days before the celebration of Passover, the chief priests and scribes were looking for a way to arrest Jesus and put him to death, but decided it was best to delay until after the festival because the people supported him. But when Judas comes along with an offer to betray him, they are delighted, and the plot is hatched (14:1–2, 10–11). After the Last Supper which Jesus shares with his disciples, Judas leads a crowd from the chief priests, scribes and elders to the Gethsemane garden, and Jesus is arrested. After his arrest Jesus is taken before the Sanhedrin to face charges; this was the supreme religious body, consisting of the high priest, all the chief priests, elders and scribes assembled together. Finally, the high priest asks Jesus whether he is the Messiah, the Son of the

Blessed One. Jesus answers clearly in the affirmative. This they dramatically interpret as blasphemy and unanimously decree that he should die (14:53–65).

Early on the following morning the chief priests, elders and scribes lead Jesus to Pilate, the Roman governor, who is in Jerusalem at Passover time. In his presence they bring many charges against him. Pilate can see that Jesus is not guilty, but the religious leaders stir up the crowd to ask for the release of a murderer named Barabbas and have Jesus put to death. They are successful, and Jesus is condemned to the hideous torture death of crucifixion (15:1–15). As Jesus hangs on the cross, the chief priests and scribes mock him: "Let the Messiah, the King of Israel, come down from the cross now, so that we may see and believe" (15:31–32). It looks as if the opposition has won the day.

Chapter Six

The End And A New Beginning

We have now reached the climax of the Gospel; in fact, Mark's Gospel is sometimes referred to as 'a passion narrative with a long introduction'. We concluded our third chapter, dedicated to the Twelve, with Jesus at the Supper predicting the betrayal by Judas, the denials by Peter and the flight of the whole group. We pick up the storyline from there. But first, a word of caution. Most Christians have a good idea of the passion story. But very often this is a kind of mosaic composed of different items from each of the evangelists. That is fine, if it helps us to pray and grow closer to Jesus. However, it does mean that we are probably unaware that actually there are three different passion stories: Mark/Matthew, Luke, and John. We also need to remember that the evangelists are not primarily interested in the details of what happened; they are concerned with the meaning of it all. Each has his own points of emphasis.

You may have noticed that most Calvary art follows John's version: Jesus is wearing a crown of thorns, his side is pierced, above his head is an inscription INRI, and his mother, the Beloved Disciple and Magdalene are standing at the foot of the cross. This is very different from Mark's presentation.

Mark's passion narrative is a really powerful piece of writing. One of his main theological themes is the isolation and loneliness of Jesus, his utter self-emptying. Jesus' earlier Supper predictions are speedily fulfilled. After the disciples have several times fallen asleep during his agony and prayer in the garden, Judas comes to the place, accompanied by a large crowd from the religious leaders armed with swords and cudgels. The man responsible for the success of the arrest is one of those singled out earlier to "be with him", a friend. His sign of betrayal is a kiss of friendship. Then every single one of the group which had shared Jesus' life together take to their heels in flight, including the youthful follower who narrowly evades capture. Despite their earlier protestations of loyalty, they are not slow to seek their own safety and leave Jesus to face his fate alone (14:43–52).

The next scene in the Passion drama comprises Jesus' 'trial' before the Sanhedrin and the denials of Peter; these two incidents are closely interlocked in Mark's account. "Then they led Jesus away to the High Priest's house, where the chief priests, elders and doctors of the law were all assembling." Already Mark has clearly designated the Jewish leaders as the ones responsible for Jesus' arrest, and he indicates each section that made up the Sanhedrin, the supreme religious and legislative body. For Mark, these are Jesus' real enemies. From the early stages of the public ministry, they have consistently opposed him, as we have seen. Now these men have Jesus in their power at last.

From the commencement of the so-called trial or inquiry, their intentions are firm and limpid; with cynical single-mindedness they "tried to find some evidence against Jesus to warrant a death sentence". Mark paints the scene in a few bold and vivid strokes: the balking incompetence of the false witnesses; the silent, dignified, isolated figure of Jesus; his foes bent unanimously on his destruction. Swiftly the evangelist brings the matter to a head, as the High Priest asks Jesus whether he is in fact the Christ, the Son of the Blessed One. For the first time in Mark's story, Jesus openly affirms that this is the case. At this, the High Priest, with an elaborate display of passionate horror, accuses him of blasphemy; and the gathering ends as planned: "they all condemned him as deserving death". Again, Mark emphasises the unanimity of the opposition and the utter aloneness of Jesus (14:53–65).

While in this atmosphere of frenzied hate and delighted success, Jesus is beaten and mocked and humiliated, Mark shifts our attention to the courtyard where Peter stands by the fire, warming himself in the chill night air. We are familiar with the painful description of Peter's triple denial of the Master. Mark skilfully orders the denials in a crescendo pattern, so that the third is the most intense, accompanied by curses and a solemn oath. Some scholars suggest that Peter, still under accusation in spite of his first two denials, resorts to the strongest possible manner of dissociating himself from Jesus by actually cursing him; this is the force to be given to that staggering disavowal: "I do not know this man you speak of", an even more emphatic restatement of his earlier rejection of Jesus' messianic way at Caesarea Philippi. Peter, singled out to be with him, decisively opts in public not to be with him. Mark heightens the effect of this by juxtaposing the incident with the trial scene: Jesus, true to himself and his mission, affirms what he cannot deny, his messiahship; and he is rejected by the religious leaders of his own people and now by his closest follower. The second cockcrow reminds Peter of Jesus' prediction, and he breaks down in tears (14:66–72).

Alone and in chains, Jesus is led away and handed over to pagan power. His rejection and isolation is further accentuated in the subsequent scene when the ordinary people shout for his death. The fickleness of crowds, the fragility of public opinion, is a commonly recognised phenomenon. From the statements of the Pharisees cited earlier in the story, it would seem that Jesus continued to enjoy a considerable amount of popularity with the masses. Yet, their acclaim was always suspect. Now, when Pilate in a desperate effort to release him, offers the mob the option of choosing Jesus Barabbas, as he was probably called, a freedom fighter convicted of murder, or Jesus of Nazareth, the crowd, incited by the chief priests, clamour for the insurrectionist and scream that Jesus be committed to the hideous torture-death of crucifixion.

We should not allow our familiarity with the story to dull our sensitivity to the poignant pain of that scene, the dreadful irony, as the nation whose whole history pointed to this moment, the nation chosen out of all peoples on the face of the earth to be God's own people (Deut 7:6ff), disowned their Emmanuel. Jesus stands there in the open, alone, the impassioned cries of the people who were his people, ringing in his ears, as they chant his rejection. His bitter desolation is intensified by a sense of injustice; even Pilate was convinced of his innocence: "Why, what harm has he done?" Then Jesus is abandoned to the Roman soldiery to be brutally scourged, made a fool of, crowned with thorns and beaten (15:2–15).

In his brief description of the crucifixion and death of Jesus, Mark emphasises the solitude of Jesus by mentioning details which, because of our acquaintance with the versions of Luke and John, we are apt to overlook. After the passers-by have hurled abuse at him and mocked him in his helpless anguish and the lawyers have jested and gibed, "even those who were crucified with him taunted him". At the end, even the robbers renounce his companionship; there is no 'good thief' here; Jesus does not belong even with his fellow sufferers. Similarly, it is only after the death of Jesus that mention is made of the women who had followed him from Galilee, and who "were watching from a distance". At the foot of the cross there is no mother, no beloved disciple; Jesus dies utterly alone.

The searing anguish of his pain and loneliness and failure is focused and captured in the loud cry from the cross: "My God, my God, why hast thou forsaken me?" Jesus' sense of abject humiliation and of total rejection by men is compounded and intensified by his feeling of being abandoned by his Father, by his experience of that estrangement and alienation that belongs to our sinfulness. He is suffocated by the intolerable pressure of evil, utterly desolate. Yet, he still calls on God as "my God" in obedient surrender. It is this surrender in the brokenness of death which, like the buried grain, is the source of our life (15:25–41).

After the death of the Baptist in Herod's prison, his disciples came, took away his body and buried it in a tomb. In the case of Jesus this service is performed by a stranger,

Joseph of Arimathea, a non-Galilean Sanhedrin member, a pious, observant Jew "waiting expectantly for the kingdom of God", the fulfilment of God's promises, but he was not a disciple. The burial is termed a "dishonourable" burial, because according to the Law Jesus is accursed; no washing or anointing took place, no lamentation. But "Mary Magdalene and Mary, mother of Joses, saw where the body was laid" (15:42–47).

However, Mark records two events which accompany the death of Jesus and are positive, redressing the balance to some extent. The first is that "the curtain of the temple was torn in two from top to bottom" (15:38). This rending of the curtain is probably to be understood, first, as symbolising the future destruction of the temple by the Romans, which had probably already taken place by the time the Gospel was written. This is seen as God's judgement of the people for their rejection of their Messiah. It also denotes the end of the temple cult and the Old Testament dispensation as a whole. The temple no longer has any religious significance. The special character which made the place a sanctuary is destroyed. The presence of God is no longer there. Secondly, more positively, the tearing of the temple veil symbolises the removal of the barrier between God and humankind; everyone now has access to a gracious God and the possibility of entering into a new relationship with God, and this includes the Gentiles, as the following episode eloquently illustrates.

The other major event consists in the response to what has occurred made by the Roman centurion responsible for the execution: "The centurion, who was standing in front of him, had seen how he had died, and he said, 'In truth this man was Son of God'" (15:39). The centurion's reaction stems from what he 'saw'. This includes Jesus' inarticulate cry and death, and possibly his last words, the surrounding darkness and the rending of the veil. It is of crucial importance that he is brought to such awareness through the death of Jesus. Neither the preaching nor the mighty works of Jesus have succeeded in penetrating the blindness and incomprehension of his disciples or the people. Jesus was condemned for blasphemy on the grounds of his messianic claim and mocked on the cross as the messianic king of Israel. It is in that total losing of self in death, that complete self-gift in the service of others that his divine sonship and the nature of his messiahship—his deepest reality—are revealed and can be understood.

The distress, darkness and horror of the story of Jesus' passion and death are lightened by the rich symbolism of the tearing of the temple veil and by the climactic comment of the centurion. These are powerful hints that the vindication hoped for by Jesus will be realised. Mark proclaims this vindication in his presentation of the events at the tomb.

With his introductory phrase, "When the Sabbath was over", Mark resumes his narrative after the silence of the Sabbath rest and links the Easter story with his description of the death and the subsequent burial of Jesus (16:1–8). The women involved are named as Mary Magdalene, Mary the mother of James, and Salome. They were present on Calvary, "looking on from a distance". Not having obtained spices on Friday, and having observed the Sabbath faithfully, the women go on Saturday evening to buy some, presumably with a view to using them next morning. Early on that Sunday morning, "the first day of the week", after the rising of the sun, they make the journey to the tomb in which Jesus was buried. Its location they know because of their presence at the burial. Because of the hurried nature of Jesus' burial, and also because it was 'dishonourable', their intention seems to be to rectify the omission. Presumably, they were also motivated by grief and loving devotion; perhaps they also sought some sort of closure. It was not unusual in that culture for relatives to visit the grave for three days after burial; in fact, mourning was at its height on the third day. Perhaps it was unrealistic of the women in such a climate to think of anointing a corpse after three days, but love and concern often override practical considerations. From their actions it is clear that they are concerned about a corpse; the possibility of Jesus' resurrection has never entered their heads.

Whilst on the way, the women wonder how they will manage to roll the stone away from the tomb entrance, given its size. As a good storyteller, Mark is creating dramatic tension and excitement, preparing for the amazing and totally unexpected surprise which follows. For, on arriving, they find the tomb open, the large stone already rolled away. The passive verb indicates the action of God; the women look up and 'see' what God has done.

Having moved inside the tomb, the women find "a young man" in a white robe, the traditional attire of heavenly beings; he is seated on the right-hand side, the position of an authoritative teacher. This figure is presumably an interpreting angel. The women are overcome with amazement and fear at this unexpected occurrence. After seeking to dispel the women's fear, the role of the angelic youth is to proclaim the Easter message: "Do not be alarmed; you are looking for Jesus of Nazareth, who was crucified. He has been raised; he is not here. Look, there is the place they laid him." The death of Jesus is not the end of his story: "He has been raised; he is not here". His faithful God and Father has not forsaken him, but has vindicated him, as Jesus had foretold, dramatically reversing his apparent failure, and conquering death. Jesus is named as "Jesus of Nazareth", as at the outset of Mark's narrative. In this way the evangelist draws together his entire story and indicates that "the Jesus whom God has raised from the dead is no other Jesus than the one with whom he began his story, namely the Jesus who is God's beloved Son."[1] The startling antithesis and contrast between "was crucified", and "was raised" by God is typical of the kerygmatic formulas and faith confessions of the early church. The insight of the centurion into the true identity of Jesus is confirmed. The formula rings out like a triumphant shout of victory. Through the angel/young man, God proclaims the resurrection of the Son. After the proclamation comes a reference to the tomb, the place where "they" had laid him, and now the reason for its emptiness becomes evident.

But Jesus' death is not the end of the story for the disciples either. The messenger continues: "But go and give this message to his disciples and Peter: 'He is going on before you into Galilee; there you will see him, as he told you.'" The women are sent on mission to the disciples, leaving the empty tomb behind. In spite of their failure and flight, their choice not to "be with" him, their unwillingness to accept the shame of belonging to him, they are still considered to be his disciples. In spite of his threefold denial, his emphatically sworn choice no longer to "be with" Jesus, Peter is still singled out for special mention.

---

1 Jack Dean Kingsbury, *The Christology of Mark's Gospel*, (Philadelphia: Fortress, 1983), 153.

The risen Lord remains faithful; he has forgiven them, and he calls them back to him once more in Galilee, as promised (14:28), where it had all begun, where they had been with him, been taught by him, witnessed his mighty deeds and had experienced mission. On the way from the supper room to Gethsemane, as in the prophet Zechariah's words, Jesus foretold his death and the fact that they would be scattered; he had also promised that he would go before them shepherd-like to Galilee. The words are here repeated with the additional assurance that they will 'see' him there. If the disciples respond to the message by following Jesus to Galilee, they will see him, see him with new eyes, come to genuine faith and clearer understanding. The scattered sheep will be gathered again, the journey of discipleship will begin anew, mission will be undertaken, especially to the Gentiles.

The final verse of Mark's gospel narrative is something of a puzzle: "So they went out and fled from the tomb, for terror and amazement had seized them; and they said nothing to anyone, for they were afraid." The women, who had remained true and stood by Jesus when all the men failed, are now overcome by fear and astonishment, terror and consternation, and they, too, take flight. Their fear is connected with the appearance and message of the "young man". In the face of God's action, a reaction of fear is not unnatural and is a common biblical feature. They are unable to cope with the experience and the news.

Their ongoing silence, expressed in a double negative, is, however, more problematic. Many scholarly explanations have been put forward. A frequently adduced view is that perhaps Mark is seeking to underline the mystery, wonder, awesomeness and supernatural character of resurrection.

Perhaps he wishes to emphasise our human inadequacy in the face of God's action. Maybe he wanted God to have the last word, the God who bestows the gift of Easter faith. "Throughout the gospel, men and women have been blind and deaf to the truth about Jesus, and now at the end, when the divine message is delivered to the women, they are struck dumb, and fail to deliver it."[2] It is Mark's final irony. Frequently, Jesus has told folk to say nothing about the truth they have glimpsed, and they have disobeyed. Now that their time has come to report what has happened, the women are silent! Even the women fail. The fearful women join the other disciples in their failure.

It is clear from the other Gospels and from Paul that the early Christian communities were aware of the appearances of the risen Jesus. Their faith was founded on this. Mark seems to have changed the story. The reader will presume that, like his other predictions and promises, this promise of Jesus, reiterated by the "young man" at the tomb, will also come true. The Christian reader knows that it did, otherwise there would be no Gospel and no believing and celebrating Christian community. Mark takes all initiative away from human beings, for they all fail; he places it with the overspilling goodness, incredible faithfulness, and gratuitous love of God. It is the Father's transforming action which has vindicated the Son's generous and loving self-gift in death. And it is the Father's action which has transformed the fearful and failed disciples and brought the Christian community into existence. Mark proclaims and articulates the faith of this community in the opening

---

2 Morna D. Hooker, *The Gospel according to St Mark*, (London; A&C Black, 1991), 387; George Martin, *The Gospel according to Mark*, (Chicago: Loyola, 2005), 452.

verse and prologue of his Gospel. His story challenges us, centuries later, to accept Jesus' way, and in our struggles and failures assures us of God's ongoing faithfulness, trustworthiness, and transforming power. We continue the story into our own lives.[3]

---

3 Most scholars believe that Mark's Gospel ends at 16:8. Later, scribes added other endings, a short one and a long one (16:9–18).

Further Reading

Boring, M. Eugene. *Mark. A Commentary.* NTL Louisville & London: Westminster John Knox, 2006.

Byrne, Brendan. *A Costly Freedom.* Collegeville, MN: Liturgical Press, 2008.

Donahue, John R. and Harrington, Daniel H. *The Gospel of Mark.* Sacra Pagina 2. Collegeville, MN: Liturgical Press, 2002.

Hooker, Morna D. *The Message of Mark.* London: Epworth Press, 1983.

__________. *The Gospel according to St. Mark.* London: A&C Black, 1991.

McBride, Denis. *The Gospel of Mark.* Dublin: Dominican Publications, 1996.

Malbon, Elizabeth S. *In the Company of Jesus: Characters in Mark's Gospel.* Louisville: Westminster John Knox, 2000.

__________. *Mark's Jesus. Characterisation as Narrative Christology.* (Wac: Baylor University Press, 2009.

Martin, George. *The Gospel according to Mark.* Chicago: Loyola, 2005.

Moloney, Francis J. *The Gospel of Mark. A Commentary.* Peabody, MA: Hendrickson, 2002.

__________. *Mark, Storyteller, Interpreter, Evangelist.* Peabody, MA: Hendrickson, 2004.

Nineham, Dennis E. *St. Mark.* London: Penguin Books, 1963.

Rhoads, David. Dewey, Joanna. Michie, Donald. *Mark as Story*. Minneapolis: Fortress, 1999.

Shiner, Whitney. *Proclaiming the Gospel: First Century Performance of Mark.* London: Continuum, 2003.

Winstanley, Michael T. *Jesus and the Little People*, Bolton: Don Bosco Publications, 2012.

__________. *Jesus and Young People*, Bolton: Don Bosco Publications, 2020.

Wright N. Tom. *Mark for Everyone.* London: SPCK, 2001.